Whatever!

NOTES

9 8 7 6 5 4 3 2 1
Digit on the right indicates the number of this printing.

ISBN 1–56138–694–4

Designed by Corinda J. Cook
Edited by Tara Ann McFadden
Printed in the United States

This book may be ordered by mail from the publisher.
Please add $1.00 for postage and handling.
But try your bookstore first!

Running Press Book Publishers
125 South Twenty-second Street
Philadelphia, Pennsylvania 19103–4399

Whatever!

NOTES

RUNNING PRESS
PHILADELPHIA • LONDON

. . . the wandering nomads of the temp world, directionless slackers. . . . They're the ones with big loans who were supposed to graduate into jobs and move out of the house but didn't, and who seem to get poorer the longer they've been away from home—unlike their parents, who seem to get richer.

Neil Howe and William Strauss
20th-century American journalists

I don't say we all ought to misbehave,
but we ought to look as if we could.

Orson Welles (1915–1985)
American film director

A good rule of thumb is if you've made it to thirty-five and your job still requires you to wear a name tag, you've probably made a serious vocational error.

DENNIS MILLER (B. 1953)
AMERICAN COMEDIAN

wendy

Everybody loves success, but they hate successful people.

John McEnroe (b. 1959)
American tennis player and commentator

If you want something abiding, something for the long run, look to failure. . . .
Real failure requires real effort, and is its own reward . . . for many years it's
failure after failure, as if we're shooting at a target but keep missing.
One day we find that failures are a kind of success.

Rafe Martin (b. 1946)
American writer

Work is the greatest thing in the world. So we should save some of it for tomorrow.

DON HEROLD (1889–1966)
AMERICAN WRITER AND ARTIST

I should have worked long enough to discover that I didn't like it.

Paul Theroux (b. 1941)
American writer

Quit now, you'll never make it. If you disregard this advice, you'll be halfway there.

David Zucker (b. 1947)
American director

The task of doing something is based upon selection and weeding out; remembering everything is weirdly similar to forgetting everything. Most things that people do shouldn't be remembered—Maybe forgetting is good.

Gary Wolfe
20th-century American writer

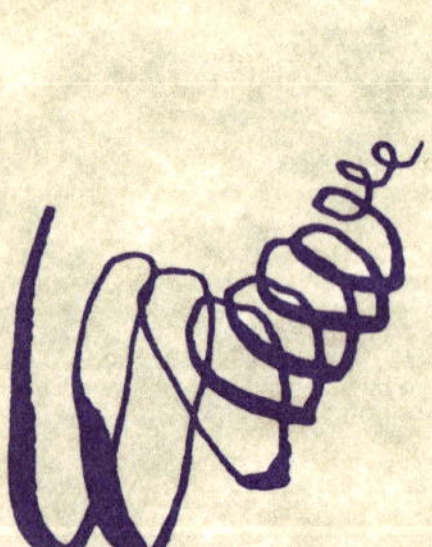

. . . if you're gonna be a failure, at least be one at something you enjoy.

Sylvester Stallone (b. 1946)
American actor, writer, and director

The day after tomorrow is the third day of the rest of your life.

George Carlin (b. 1937)
American comedian

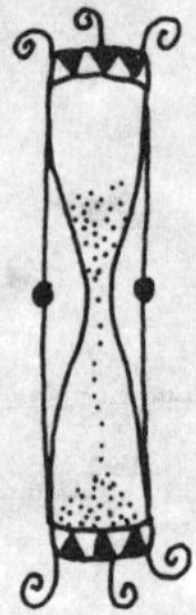

The worst thing about television is that everybody you see on television is doing something better than what you're doing.

Jerry Seinfeld (b. 1954)
American comedian and writer

Television is more interesting than people.

If it were not, we should have people standing in the corners of our rooms.

ALAN COREN (B. 1938)
ENGLISH HUMORIST

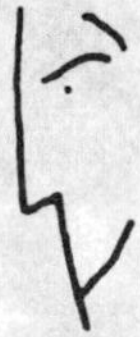

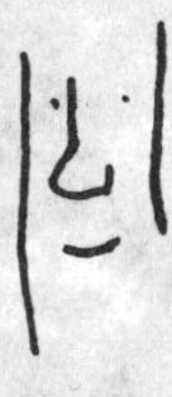

We are so vain that we even care for the opinion of those we don't care for.

Marie von Ebner-Eschenbach (1830–1916)
Austrian writer

A narcissist is someone better looking than you are.

Gore Vidal (b. 1925)
American writer and playwright

The human species, according to the best theory I can form of it, is composed of two distinct races, those who borrow and those who lend.

CHARLES LAMB (B. 1926)
AMERICAN ARCHITECT

Getting caught is the mother of invention.

Robert Byrne (b. 1930)
American writer

. . . to me the outdoors is what you must pass through
in order to get from your apartment into a taxicab.

Fran Lebowitz (b. 1950)
American writer

The only stability is in accepting uncertainty.

Pierre A. Wack
20th-century American writer

The only way to be absolutely safe is never to try anything for the first time.

Magus Pyke (b. 1908)
English scientist and writer

Answering the question is not nearly as interesting as reading it would be.

NEIL YOUNG (B. 1945)
AMERICAN SINGER AND SONGWRITER

When we remember we are all mad, the mysteries of life disappear and life stands explained.

Mark Twain (1835–1910)
American writer

Life is like an overlong drama through which we sit being nagged by the vague memories of having read the reviews.

John Updike (b. 1932)
American writer

What if everything is an illusion and nothing exists?

In that case, I definitely overpaid for my carpet.

Woody Allen (b. 1935)
American filmmaker

This is what it's all about: If you can't have fun at it, there's no sense hanging around.

Joe Montana (b. 1956)
American football player

If you can't dazzle them with brilliance baffle them with mood swings.

Wayne R. Guevara
20th-century American cashier

Thinking is the hardest work there is,

which is the probable reason why so few engage in it.

HENRY FORD (1863–1947)
AMERICAN INDUSTRIALIST

I like the weirdo tag. It's quite flattering

because it makes me seem more interesting than I am. . . .

Björk (b. 1966)
Icelandic-born American singer and songwriter

If you talk brilliantly about a problem, it can create the consoling illusion that it has been mastered.

STANLEY KUBRICK (B. 1928)
AMERICAN DIRECTOR

A word to the wise ain't necessary—it's the stupid ones who need the advice.

Bill Cosby (b. 1937)
American comedian, actor, and writer

The very purpose of existence is to reconcile the glowing opinion we hold of ourselves with the appalling things that other people think about us.

QUENTIN CRISP
20TH-CENTURY AMERICAN WRITER

I certainly hope that when I'm fifty, I won't be thinking about having plastic surgery to buy me another five or six years. But you never know. . . .

Molly Ringwald (b. 1968)
American actress

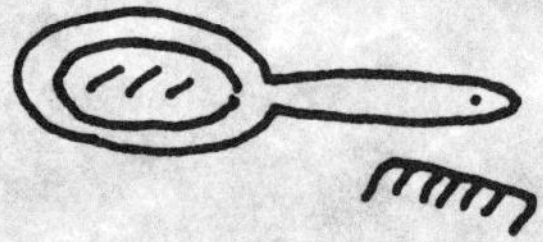

To fall in love with yourself is the first secret of happiness. I did so at the age of 4½. Then if you're not a good mixer you can always fall back on your own company.

Robert Morley (1908–1992)
English actor

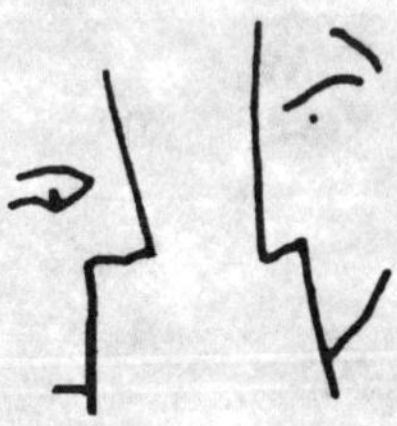

Don't talk about yourself; it will be done when you leave.

ADDISON MIZNER (1872–1933)
AMERICAN ARCHITECT AND WRITER

If you're going to do something wrong, at least enjoy it.

Leo Rosten (b. 1908)
Polish writer

Anything can change, without warning, and that's why I try not to take any of what's happened too seriously.

Donald Trump (b. 1946)
American businessman

As soon as you get an image, you gotta break it.

Brad Pitt
20th-century American actor

When in doubt, make a fool of yourself. There is a microscopically thin line between being brilliantly creative and acting like the most gigantic idiot on earth. So what the hell, leap.

Cynthia Heimel (b. 1947)
American writer

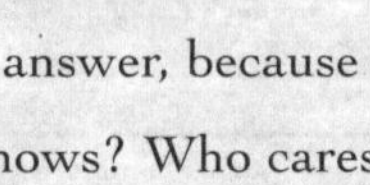

. . . what is GenX? There's no answer, because that's an ignorant boomer question. Who knows? Who cares? Whatever.

Mark Saltveit
20th-century writer and executive